The author would like to dedicate this book to
John Crompton (John Battersby Crompton Lamburn (1893 – 1972)
for his wonderful book
"Ways of the Ant"

When I read this book two decades ago, I was amazed at the complex behaviours of various species of ants. I wondered why I had never learned about such interesting creatures when I was a child. John Crompton's narrative style was delightful, and made the book not only immensely readable, but also entertaining. His book was an inspiration for this children's picture book, which I hope will entertain kids while introducing them to one very interesting species of ant.

The author would like to thank those family members, friends and colleagues who have given their encouragement and support for this project.

A special thanks goes to Roberto González Lara
roberto@rogolart.com | www.rogolart.com
for his wonderful creativity and expertise in illustrating and formatting this book.

A Strange Guest in an Ant's Nest

Printed in the USA

ISBN: 978-0993800344

A Strange Guest in an Ant's Nest

By Sharon Clark

Illustrated by Roberto González

The countryside appeared peaceful on that warm, summer afternoon. Tall green weeds and yellow grasses swayed gently in the breeze. The sky was a deep blue with an occasional fluffy white cloud drifting past. Though the scene appeared quiet and calm, it hid the activities of thousands of busy creatures hurriedly going about their daily business.

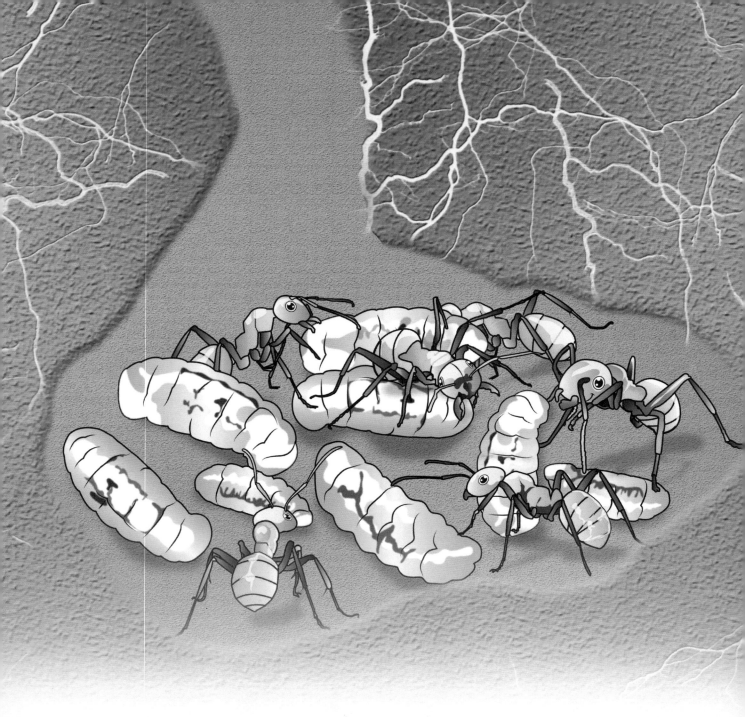

Amber, a pale yellow meadow ant, was still full of curiosity at
everything around her. She had emerged just two days before
from her cocoon and had been amazed at the world she had
entered. She found herself in a deep nest underground with
thousands of other ants. Each one was busy with some activity.
She quickly learned how to perform her duties as a worker
in the colony.

Before long she was helping her sister workers care for the eggs that her queen mother had laid. The larvae inside were beginning their worm-like form of ant development. They were very delicate and needed specific temperature and moisture in order to survive. So, Amber watched how her sisters moved them. Then she carefully picked up one egg at a time in her mouth and carried it gently to a good location in the nest. During the day, she would help her sisters transport each one closer to the surface of the nest where the eggs would be warmed by the sun's rays. At night, as the outside air cooled, she would help them transport each one deeper into the nest where the internal temperature was warmer.

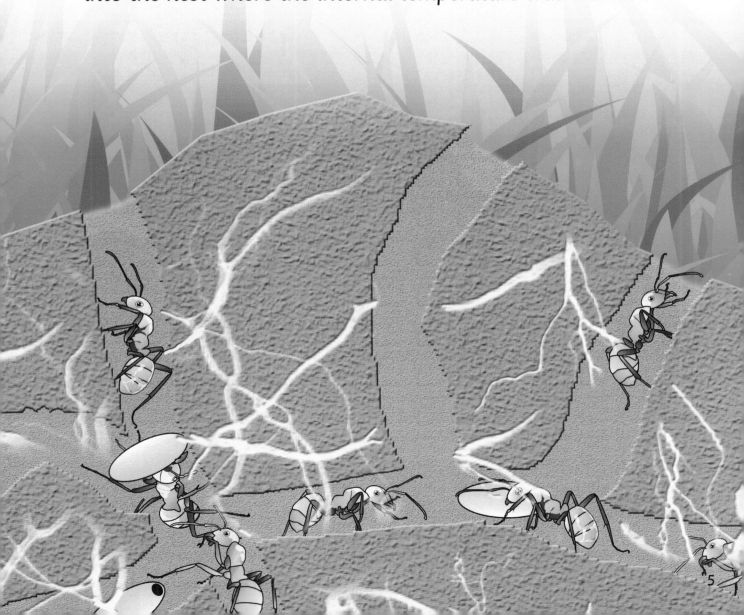

Now, for the moment, Amber's work was done. She rested in one of the many underground chambers and took some time to groom herself. One by one she cleaned each of her six legs. But, as she began to clean the first of her two antennae, these sensors suddenly detected a strong smell. Her little heart began to pound. Amber knew that this particular scent was an alarm signal. She had encountered it once before and it had caused her sisters to become very excited. So she bolted to attention, alert to any danger.

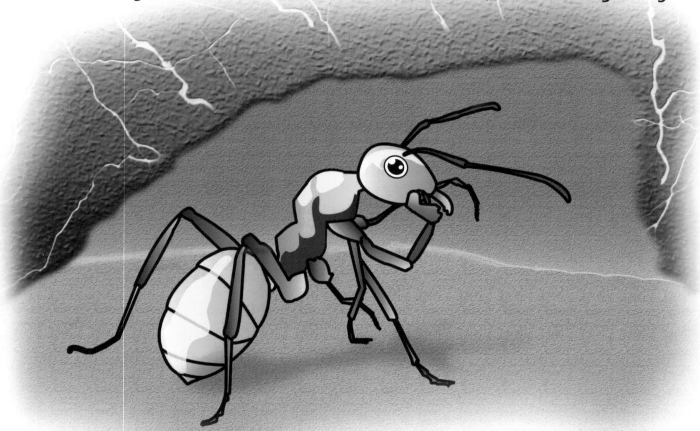

Suddenly, frantic ants filled the chamber she was in. Small workers that looked like her rushed past and quickly headed deeper underground. Larger worker ants also appeared, but they did not follow the others. Instead, they headed up tunnels that lead to the surface of the nest. They were preparing for battle. Amber began to follow the larger ants because she was curious to see the enemy. But something made her stop. Instinct told her that she was needed elsewhere. The eggs needed to be protected at all costs.

6

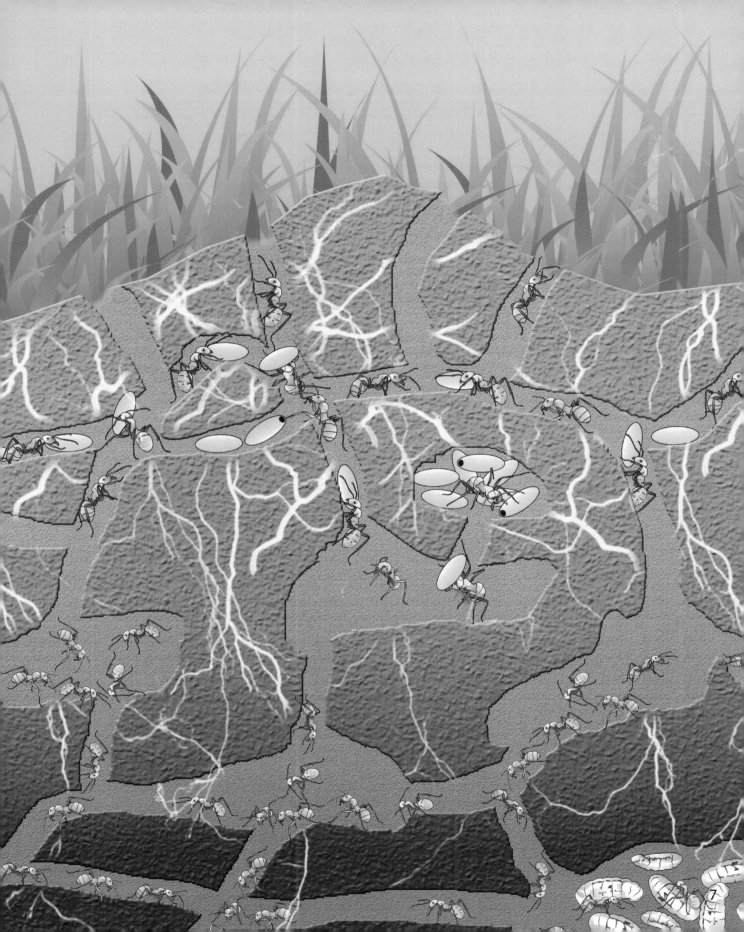

So, Amber turned and ran deeper into the nest. Once she joined the others, she began helping her sisters move the eggs to a safer location. Then they stood guard over their precious charges and prepared to battle any enemy that might appear. However, after a short while, the alarm scents began to decrease. One by one, the larger ants re-entered the nest. Most of them returned unharmed. The battle must have been over quickly. Worker ants began caring for the ones that were injured. They brought them food and licked their wounds.

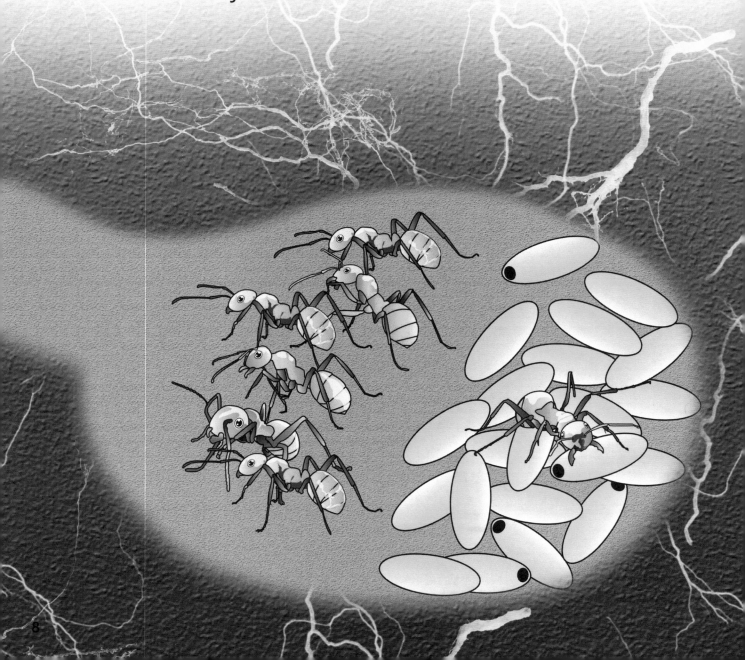

Soon, the colony resumed its usual activities. Amber returned to grooming her antennae. But, before long, a new scent filled the air. She looked up eagerly, now realizing how hungry she was! Some workers had returned carrying insect parts. Ants gathered all around them, excitedly anticipating a tiny piece. Amber quickly joined them. When the flesh was placed before them they each tore off a tiny chunk. It was very satisfying, so she ate heartily.

After eating, Amber felt quite refreshed. It was now time to resume her duties. Some larvae had hatched from the eggs that day and they were hungry too. She needed to follow the scent trail laid by the larger workers. Perhaps the previous battle with ants from other nests had left many dead enemies. Their flesh would give the larvae the protein they needed or grow and develop into mature ants. As soon as Amber bent her antennae towards the ground, she quickly picked up the trail. Up, up through tunnels she went until suddenly, she was in the outside world for the first time in her short life.

Amber was dazed by the brightness of her new surroundings. Until now, she had only lived in darkness. What she saw with her two compound eyes and three simple eyes amazed her. This was the first time that she had seen objects in colour. Various shades of yellows and greens were all around her. She stared at a plant in front of her, then her eyes followed its stalk upward. The plant rose high above her, until it was seen on the background of a brilliant blue sky. Amber stared at this new colour for a very long while. She became so absorbed in this new world that she almost forgot why she was there. Then one of her sisters rushed past her with an insect part. Dutifully, Amber bent her antennae downward and resumed her exploration of the scent trail.

Before long, she came upon the battle scene. Little black ants lay dead in a clearing. Many of her sisters were using their sharp teeth to rip off pieces of meat. Then they hurried back to the nest to feed the larvae and queen. Amber began to help, making many trips to and from the nest. Every trip was uneventful. But then it happened!

At first Amber did not see it because she was looking downward.
Then, suddenly, she noticed a huge shadow in her path.
Instinctively, her eyes shot upward and she couldn't understand
what she was seeing. A strange green creature stood before her.
She had never seen anything like it! The beast reared up on its front
legs and stuck out its belly. When more of these critters appeared,
Amber's heart began to race and she filled the air with alarm scents.
Soon her larger sisters were at her side.

Even with the arrival of the larger ants, the creature remained upright and motionless. Amber prepared to witness a fierce battle! But to her surprise, the other ants didn't attack. They did not produce alarm scents either, even though they did seem very excited. To Amber's amazement and confusion, one of her sisters approached the beast and began stroking its belly with her antenna. Then this ant also began to tap the beast's belly as if it were a drum. The creature was an aphid and it seemed to love the attention! Its body began to relax and sag. Whenever the ant's stroking stopped, the aphid presented its belly for more. Amber could not believe what she was seeing!

As the stroking and tapping ritual continued, a clear drop of fluid slowly emerged from the aphid's body. The ant swallowed some of this sweet liquid, often called honeydew. She seemed to enjoy this liquid because she waited for more. Other ants moved closer so they too could have a taste. As soon as they drank the liquid, they became very calm and content. Amber hesitated but then she was overcome by curiosity. She sampled the clear liquid. It was amazing! In fact, it was the most pleasant food she had ever tasted and a sense of calm and contentment swept over her. Over and over, the ants lined up for more, until eventually, the clear liquid was gone. Then an even more amazing thing happened!.

The aphid slowly began to arch it's back. An ant quickly moved underneath. It used its mouthparts to pick it up. Amber was curious to know what her sister was doing. She couldn't take her eyes off of the scene before her. The larger worker ant now began carrying the aphid in the direction of Amber's nest. The creature didn't protest. Amber was puzzled, so she began to follow. Other ants joined in. As they approached the entrance to the nest, other workers greeted them excitedly. Amber watched in disbelief as her sisters disappeared into their nest with this strange creature.

When her sisters or the aphid did not return, Amber followed them into her nest. She noticed the scent her sisters left and it helped her find which direction they went. Soon she entered a long downward tunnel. These were new surroundings. Down, down she went, following the tunnel's twists and turns. Suddenly, Amber entered a huge chamber that she had never been in before. She couldn't believe the sight before her!

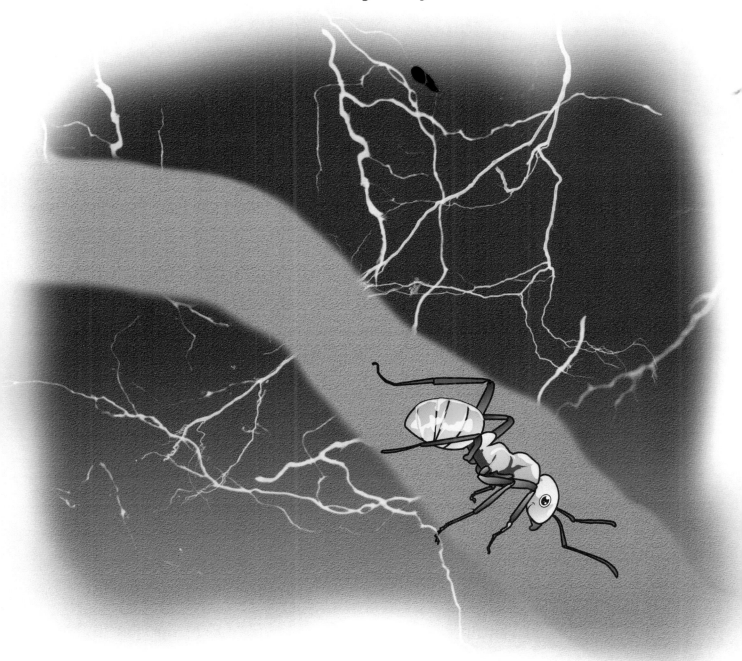

Roots of plants were coming through the chamber's ceiling. And aphids were everywhere! Some were sucking sap from the plant's roots. Others were being stroked by ants and were giving honeydew. And some were being groomed by ants to make sure that the aphids were kept clean. Amber stood for a very long while, taking in the scene before her. Until today, she had only seen ants in her nest. But, now she found other creatures, so very different from her, living in harmony with all of them. Here was a scene of peace and contentment. Both aphids and ants seemed to find it perfectly natural to be in each other's company!

Amber was not able to understand why this relationship benefited both creatures. The aphids were content because they were treated like special guests. They never had to search for food because the ants brought them to the plant roots that they liked to feed on. They also could live in a cozy, dry and warm environment. They were safe from enemies and the ants kept them clean and healthy. Furthermore, they loved the stroking. The ants too were happy with this arrangement. Their guests provided them with a constant supply of delicious and nourishing food. This was especially important over the long, cold winter months when food was so scarce.

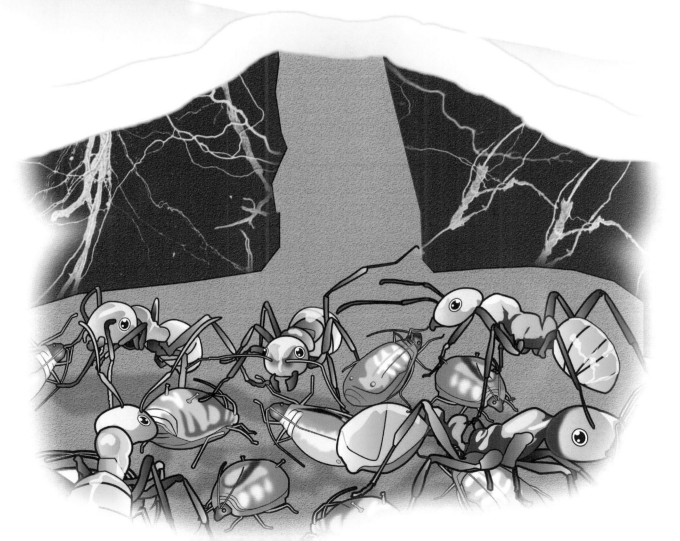

Amber stared in wonder for a long while. Her world was different now, yet she felt very contented. Though these strange new guests at first seemed odd and scary, they made her home a far richer place in which to live.

Other Books
by **Sharon Clark** and **Roberto González**

This clever little mouse teaches kids a fun and easy way to learn the 9X table.

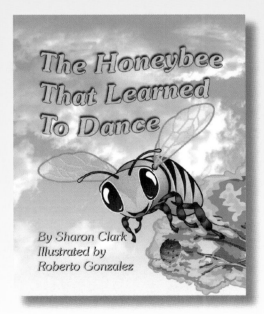

Interesting behaviours of honeybees demonstrated through Hummy's first day as a forager.

Making Math and Science **FUN** for Kids

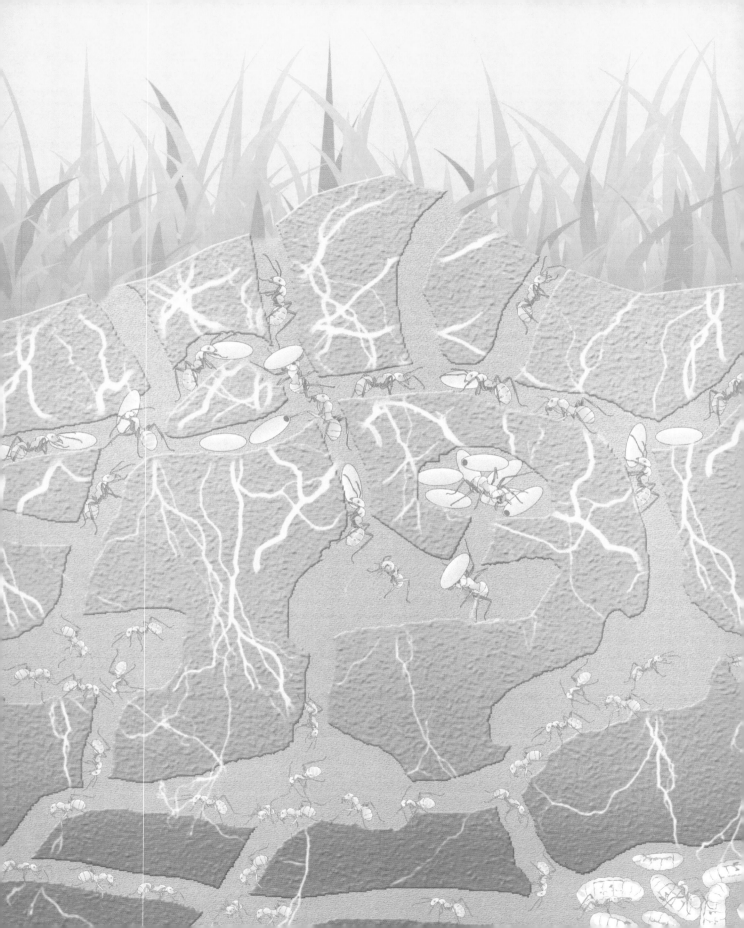